Norman Carrington MA

C000220293

Brodie's Notes on Shaw's

Pygmalion

Timothy is edible!

Pan Books London and Sydney

To the student

A close reading of the play is the student's primary
task. These Notes will help to increase your understanding
and appreciation of the play, and to stimulate *your own*
thinking about it. *They are in no way intended as a substitute*
for a thorough knowledge of the play – of which, if possible,
you would find it helpful to attend a performance.

First published by James Brodie Ltd
This edition published 1976 by Pan Books Ltd
Cavaye Place, London SW10 9PG

9

© James Brodie Ltd 1974
ISBN 0330 50033 3
Filmset in Great Britain by
Northumberland Press Ltd, Gateshead, Tyne and Wear
Printed and bound by
Richard Clay (The Chaucer Press) Ltd, Bungay, Suffolk

This book is sold subject to the condition that it
shall not, by way of trade or otherwise, be lent, re-sold,
hired out, or otherwise circulated without the publisher's prior
consent in any form of binding or cover other than that in which
it is published and without a similar condition including this
condition being imposed on the subsequent purchaser

Contents

These Notes are based on the Penguin Plays edition
of *Pygmalion* but as each Act is referred to and
analysed separately, the Notes may be used with any
edition of the play.

The
London
of
Pygmalion

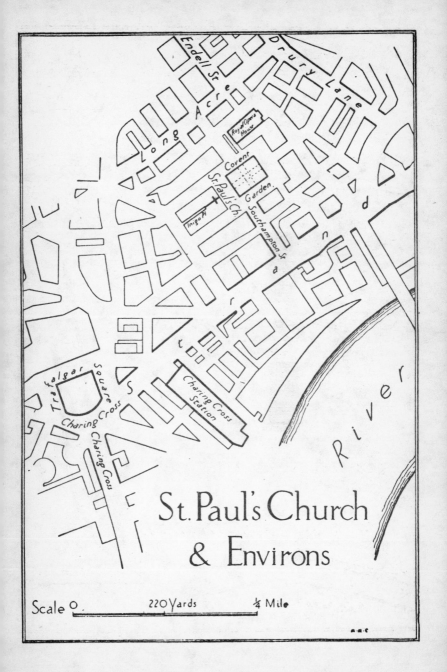

Endell Str.

Drury Lane

Long Acre

Royal Opera House

Covent Garden

St. Paul's Ch.

Inigo Pl.

Southampton Str.

Strand

Trafalgar Square

Charing Cross

Charing Cross

Charing Cross Station

River

St. Paul's Church
& Environs

Scale 0.　　　220 Yards　　　¼ Mile

I lay my eternal curse on whomsoever shall now or at any time hereafter make schoolbooks of my works, and make me hated, as Shakespear is hated. My plays were not designed as instruments of torture.

Bernard Shaw,
in a letter dated 24 November 1927

The author and his work

George Bernard Shaw, the most provocative controversialist of the first half of the twentieth century, was born in Dublin on 26 July 1856. It was a poor and an unhappy home. His father made an indifferent sort of living as a corn broker, but the family made ends meet by taking in a teacher of singing, called Lee, as a paying guest. Lee discovered that Shaw's mother had a beautiful mezzo-soprano voice which he trained. But when after some years he sought his fortune in London, the Shaw family were left with a house they could not afford on their hands. Mrs Shaw gave up the unequal struggle and, following Lee's example, set off for London with her two daughters (both older than Bernard) in 1871. She established herself as a teacher of singing and music, leaving her fifteen-year-old son and his father to go into lodgings.

The boy had lessons from a clergyman uncle and eventually entered the Wesleyan Connexional School, Dublin (now Wesley College). His entry in *Who's Who* in his lifetime read, 'Educated at Wesley College, Dublin, *and other boy prisons.*' From all accounts he was none too satisfactory a pupil, but this should not be taken too seriously, as great men tend to belittle their education. Regardless of what he may or may not have gained from his years at school, it is clear that Shaw owed more to the appreciation of music and painting inherited from his mother and indeed to his own love of reading. He read anything and everything that came his way, not only children's classics like *The Arabian Nights*, *The Pilgrim's Progress* and *Robinson Crusoe*, but *The Faerie Queene*, the poems of Byron and most of the novels of Scott and Dickens.

At fifteen years of age Shaw was apprenticed to a Dublin land agent. His ability was obvious from the first and a year later he became the firm's cashier, replacing a man of forty! But the thought of spending his life at an office desk weighed him down. As the years wore on he could not stand it, and in 1876 he left and joined his mother in London.

It was not an easy time for a man to begin a new career. In that year a slump hit the country such as it was not to see again until 1931, and people had no money to spend on books and magazines. He spent nine years in hack-writing and odd jobs for business firms, and during this time, he tells us, he made no more than £5 9s. 6d. (£5.47½) by his pen. In between times, to quote his own words, 'I made a man of myself (at my mother's expense) instead of a slave.' He wrote five novels, none of which was published; his explanation was that his style was a hundred and fifty years behind the times and his ideas a hundred and fifty years ahead of them! It was nearly fifty years before his justly named first novel, *Immaturity*, was published. Once he had made a name for himself as a playwright publishers were clamouring for anything he could give them – they were sure of a sale because the book bore his name. The other four novels were *Cashel Byron's Profession* (generally reckoned to be the best), *The Irrational Knot*, *The Unsocial Socialist* and *Love Among the Artists*. They were all written in businesslike fashion – so many pages a day, come wet or fine. But Shaw will not have it that he ever had to 'struggle' for a living. Looking back on his career, Shaw declared, 'I never struggled, I rose by sheer gravitation.'

Be that as it may, it was not until he turned to criticism that Shaw made any headway. He became acquainted with William Archer, one of the reviewers of *The Pall Mall Gazette*, and at one time when he was hard-pressed Archer gave Shaw a book to review. This review set him off on his career, and after that he had as much book reviewing for *The Pall Mall Gazette* as he cared to do, at two guineas per thousand words. He made £112 in his first year as a critic. Archer was also theatre critic for *The World*, and on the death of the art critic, Archer was asked to take on the job. Archer knew nothing about pictures, and so recommended Shaw who became art critic to *The World* at fivepence a line. In 1885 he became music critic of *The Star*, under the pseudonym of Corno di Bassetto (the name of an obsolete musical instrument) at two guineas a week. He was now finding a practical use for the appreciation of painting and music which he had inherited from his mother. The student will notice his sure and easy touch when talking of pictures in the stage direction at the beginning of Act 3 of *Pygmalion*, and (less clearly) his knowledge of music in the conversation at the end of the Act. After two years Corno di Bassetto became music critic to *The World* also and now earned £5 a week for contributions to the two papers. The word 'brilliant' was now being freely applied to his work. Before very long he felt sure enough of himself to discard his pseudonym and sign his articles G.B.S. Not only was his work well-spoken of, but he was business-like, and one thing that won him commendation from editors was that he was always on time with his articles. In the early nineties he became the drama critic of *The Saturday Review*; in addition to his regular weekly articles, he contributed from time to time other reviews of books and pictures for the papers with which he was associated. His money troubles were now at an end.

But it was his spare-time activities that gave zest to his life rather than the daily round and common task. He studied Karl Marx and became a prominent figure in the early Socialist movement. In 1884 he was one of the founder members of the Fabian Society. He always regarded himself a Socialist, but at this time he 'worked at it' – writing innumer-

able Fabian tracts and speaking on Fabian platforms (sometimes two or three times a day). Two of his early plays, *Widowers' Houses* and *Mrs. Warren's Profession*, have a Socialist flavour, but his Socialist view-point was kept out of his later plays. In 1928, he gave his political creed a volume to itself in *The Intelligent Woman's Guide to Socialism and Capitalism*. But, as in everything else, Shaw is essentially individual, and his beliefs cannot be identified with those of any one political party; indeed in their heyday he expressed admiration of Lenin, Mussolini and Hitler with equal fervour. But in the eighties and nineties of the last century he identified himself closely with the growing Socialist movement, and grudged every minute he was not working for it. Later he became something of a capitalist by selling the world unpleasant truths about itself that it did not want to know but was eager to buy. One of his fads at this time was living on greens and water, and the result of continual hard work on a diet like this was that in 1898 he had a complete breakdown. His recovery was due to the attentions of the 'heroic lady' whom he married when he was better, Charlotte Frances Payne-Townshend. He never again engaged actively in political propaganda.

Shaw is the only modern dramatist who started to write plays which were *read* and not *acted*. For nearly two years most of his plays were published but not acted. All his plays are problem plays and were read as much for the prefaces as for the plays themselves. It was 1904 before his plays were produced regularly although *Widowers' Houses*, his first, was produced at the Royalty Theatre in 1892, but without much success. It later made a hit in Berlin after the first world-war. Socialists in England welcomed it as propaganda, but in those early days Socialism was regarded as the creed of a few extremists and the general public turned a cold shoulder. That, of course, is the reason why it was written. Shaw intended to use the theatre for propaganda. He declared that the man who believed in art for art's sake is a fool, a hopeless fool, and in a state of 'damnation'. *Widower's Houses* is an attack on the slum evil in our cities. Trench is the type who is an idealist only so long as his idealism does not empty his pocket, and like Dickens and Thackeray and Galsworthy, Shaw sees through the snobbery and hypocrisy of social life, and he unveils it more ruthlessly than any. Even *Pygmalion*, which no one would think of interpreting as propaganda had he not read the Preface, is, Shaw says 'intensely and deliberately didactic'. Whereas most people think of *Pygmalion*, in the words of one critic, as a play of 'intelligent gaiety' Shaw's motive (if his Preface can be believed) is a narrowly didactic one.

If the play makes the public aware that there are such people as phoneticians and that they are among the most important in England at present, it well serves its turn ... It is so intensely and deliberately didactic ... that I delight in throwing it at the heads of wiseacres who repeat the parrot cry that art should never be didactic. It goes to prove my contention that art should never be anything else (Preface to *Pygmalion*).

Arms and the Man, Shaw's second play, ran for eleven weeks at the Avenue Theatre in 1894, but only to half-full houses. Here he tilts at romance – romance in warfare. Romance is false. Shaw sees life as it is, without qualification, compromise or sparing anyone's feelings. In *Man and Superman* the idea that woman is the pursued and man the pursuer, the conventional belief, is shown to hide the reality. *How he Lied to Her Husband* is another tilt at romance. Romantic convention assumes that husbands are jealous admirers of their wives. Mr Bompas, her husband, gets angry only when Henry, his wife's lover, pretends he has no love for her. Things are turned inside out again, and our conventional ideas are swept away by the author's delightful wit and paradox. Whatever the faith of the public Shaw was certain to enjoy pulling it to pieces. People take it for granted that man has progressed immeasurably since the days of Caesar and Cleopatra. In *Caesar and Cleopatra* Shaw makes us realize that in those days people reacted to things exactly as they do now. The public believes implicitly what it is told by doctors. Shaw must unmask them in *The Doctor's Dilemma*. The public believes that Joan of Arc was a saint, grossly wronged by the wicked men of her day and generation, but in *Saint Joan* he shows that if she appeared on earth today people would look at her in exactly the same light as our ancestors did five centuries ago. Shaw believed that human nature could not be changed: Cleopatra remains a savage despite Caesar's efforts to improve her; Ferrovius cannot forbear slaying the gladiators, although full of an inward resolve to follow Christ his master.

Between 1892 and 1940 Shaw wrote no fewer than fifty plays (roughly one a year), and until he was seventy there was no decline in either his mental energy or his creative impulse. Among the best known of his plays written during this period are: *Mrs Warren's Profession*, *Arms and the Man* and *Candida* (all published in 1898); *Caesar and Cleopatra* and *Captain Brassbound's Conversion* (both 1901); *Man and Superman* (1902); *John Bull's Other Island* (1904); *Major Barbara* (1905); *The Doctor's Dilemma* (1906); *Pygmalion* (1912), adapted as the successful musical play *My Fair Lady* (1956) and the film of the same name (1964); *Androcles and the Lion* (1913); *Saint Joan* (1923); *The Apple Cart* (1929); and *The Millionairess* (1936).

The best work of most authors has been produced in the prime of life: *Saint Joan*, reckoned by most people to be Shaw's masterpiece, was written when he was nearly seventy. It strikes every chord from happy laughter to poignant tragedy. It enjoyed an immense success in New York in 1923, and again in London in 1924, with Sybil Thorndike in the title part. Shaw was awarded the Nobel Prize for Literature in 1926 (six years before Galsworthy). In his earlier plays the theme generally has a slant towards economic affairs, but in the later plays the emphasis is a religious one. Edmund Wilson says that Shaw's plays 'have been a truthful and continually developing chronicle of a soul in relation to society'. In that case the change is significant. *Saint Joan* and *Androcles and the Lion* bring religious views into prominence. To state Shaw's constant beliefs on *anything* is difficult, most of all his religious beliefs: he liked to pose as an enigma and consequently whatever statement is made about his beliefs can be contradicted somewhere in his work. 'I say that Life Force is God,' he wrote; and perhaps St John Ervine best summarizes Shaw's religous outlook;

God, or the Life Force, is an imperfect power striving to become perfect ... The whole of time has been occupied by God in experiments with instruments invented to help Him in His attempt to perfect Himself. God created a new instrument, Man, who is still on probation. Shaw warns the world that if we, too, fail to achieve God's purpose He will become impatient and scrap mankind as He scrapped the mammoth beasts.

In the main Shaw's plays have been kept alive in England by Repertory Companies and stage societies, though there have been long runs with star actors. Barry Jackson, the proprietor of the Birmingham Repertory Theatre, in association with John Drinkwater (the author of *Abraham Lincoln*) did as much to bring out Shaw as anyone. He made a success of *Heartbreak House* (which Shaw called his best play) at the Birmingham Rep and, to everyone's amazement, of the long play *Back to Methuselah*, which took five nights to perform. *Arms and the Man* was produced in New York after London and since 1910 Shaw's plays have been produced regularly in USA. He swore he would never set foot in USA, but he did make a brief visit on his world tour in 1938.

Pygmalion was Shaw's first theatrical success in a large commercial theatre (though *Fanny's First Play* had had a long and successful run at a Repertory Theatre. It is his most characteristic if not his greatest play. It was written in 1912, and was produced abroad many times before it was shown in England. By 11 April 1914, when it was produced by Sir Herbert Beerbohm Tree at His Majesty's Theatre, London, it had been performed in Berlin, New York, Vienna, Stockholm, Prague, Warsaw and Budapest, and translated as a play in book form in most of the countries of which these cities are the capitals. It ran in London until the third week of July, and later the company toured USA with it. After the war it was revived at the Aldwych Theatre (1920). Since then it has made an appearance in Italy, Spain and Mexico. 'I wish to boast,' wrote Shaw in the Preface, 'that Pygmalion has been an extremely successful play all over Europe and North America as well as at home.'

The stir caused by Eliza's phrase 'not bloody likely' on a London stage helped the play's popularity. Nowadays we are accustomed to hear the expletive 'bloody' in stage and radio performances, and it is difficult to imagine the shock with which it came over in 1912, though it was neither the first nor the second time the word had been heard from the stage of a theatre. Perhaps it will help the student to realize the shock it caused by saying that in the reviews of the play not one newspaper printed the word; they all by-passed it with some such euphemism as 'the sanguinary expletive'. Letters (invariably in emphatic protest) poured in to the Press. This did Shaw good. People who would never have thought of seeing a Shaw play read the letters and wanted to go and see *Pygmalion*. This was a pity, for it took the interest of the play away from the clever situation and brilliant wit on to a passing trifle. The use of the word is perfectly in keeping with Eliza's character and background, and its incongruity in the company in which it is uttered still creates a burst of laughter at every performance.

In 1929 Sir Barry Jackson arranged a festival of Shaw's plays at Malvern, inaugurated by a new play, *The Apple Cart*. Shaw was in his element 'at the festival, walking about the town wearing odd clothes, doing eccentric things, expressing controversial opinions, and generally enjoying a public adulation second only to that given to film stars. He was of a very different temperament from Galsworthy, who never cared to talk of the success of his plays and always tried to change the subject if it was mentioned. But Shaw was living on his reputation – *The Apple Cart* was feeble by the side of *Saint Joan*: at the best it is second-rate Shaw. Sir Barry Jackson continued the festival the following year, but it was not an all-Shavian programme, and in 1931 he was dropped altogether.

In one way Shaw resembled Galsworthy – he was strongly opposed to having any of his plays filmed, and for a long time withstood all entreaties and bribes. Eventually, however, he gave way, and in 1938 *Pygmalion* was the first of his plays to be filmed. Characteristically enough, after having refused to allow a film of one of his plays to be made, when filming began Shaw himself supervised its production. It is not generally known that about 1912 Shaw acted as a cowboy in a film for Barrie. After a dinner party of literary men given by Mr Asquith, at the Savoy Hotel, Shaw, Chesterton, Barrie, and one or two others went down to Elstree and rigged themselves up as cowboys. Then they did all sorts of insane things – chased horses, rode motor-cycles and crawled in and out of drainpipes. In one scene Shaw had to ride over a 'precipice' with five people behind him on a motor-cycle. Unfortunately, however, Barrie scrapped the film. Whatever its success might have been as a film it would certainly have been interesting as a commentary on the leisure-time activities of literary men!

The film of *Pygmalion* followed Sir Beerbohm Tree's first stage production of the play in England, and in spite of Shaw's objections to this interpretation (see the Epilogue) he was unable to prevent the film turning into the romantic love story of a girl from the slums who became a lady and married the man who transformed her. The play as we have it is more in character. Because the Pygmalion of classical mythology married his statue, this does not mean that Shaw intended to follow the classical Pygmalion story at every point, in defiance of the character in his play – and indeed he disclaims this in the Epilogue. Film producers are out to make money, and clearly the filmed *Pygmalion*, even though more improbable than the play, would, with this romantic twist, have greater appeal for cinema audiences. As a result of the success of *Pygmalion* as a film, negotiations began for the rights to film others of Shaw's plays when the war caused the project to be shelved. However, after the war *Caesar and Cleopatra* and *Saint Joan* both appeared as films, and both were truer to their play original than *Pygmalion*.

In 1956 a musical version of *Pygmalion* called *My Fair Lady* was the rage of New York and set up a Broadway record (at the box office) in its first year; in 1964, this highly successful musical play was made into a film with Rex Harrison and Audrey Hepburn in the star roles.

No modern playwright has had so much trouble with the censor as Shaw, though it is within the bounds of possibility that much of it has been engineered for its publicity value. It may surprise many students to know that *Saint Joan* was at first banned by the British censors on religious grounds. It is equally surprising that Shaw was not censored during the last World War when he made many un-patriotic statements. Perhaps the reason was that the authorities were never quite

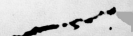

sure when he was serious and were afraid of his turning the tables on them if they interfered with him. Shaw's wartime article *The Cops Won't Let Me Talk!* was a pathetic outburst, and had it been written by anyone else but Shaw it would never have seen daylight. But an article by George Bernard Shaw, of course, (especially one with such a provocative title) had great sales value.

Shaw was his own publicity agent. He always believed that it pays to advertise. Modesty was not one of his strong points, as the reader has seen from quotation from the Preface to *Pygmalion*.

In England, as elsewhere, the spontaneous recognition of really original work begins with a mere handful of people and propagates itself so slowly that it has become a commonplace to say that genius, demanding bread, is given a stone after its possessor's death. The remedy for this is sedulous advertisement. Accordingly, I have advertised myself so well that I find myself almost as legendary a person as the Flying Dutchman.

One cannot quarrel with what he says usually, the only thing is that it would sound better coming from somebody else. The tone of many passages such as the one quoted makes one wonder how far they are to be taken seriously. A lot of this sort of talk was bravado: Shaw set himself up as a crank and had to live the part. That is the reason why so many contradictory things have been said about him, all of which can be substantiated from his work. In his seemingly most earnest moments we can never be quite sure that he is not 'pulling our leg', and indeed Shaw delighted in his public's bewilderment. Thus to one he is a great man of genius, while to another he is a sheer humbug.

Some of Shaw's friendships have been bizarre for a man of letters. In 1929, when he was over seventy, he went for a holiday with Gene Tunney, the boxer, in Italy (a country at that time under the rule of one of Shaw's heroes). The only thing they seemed to have in common was that (in different ways) they both knew how to hit out. Shaw was, however, interested in prize-fighters in boyhood and in his youth had himself a reputation as a fighter of some note. After that he became a fighter in another sense and spent his life 'knocking spots off people' with his pen.

Shaw himself was convinced that he would be 'a panjam-drum of literature for the next three hundred years'. That remains to be seen. Joseph Woodkrutch, the American author, has a very different view:

'It was chiefly as a stimulant that he was valuable.... A showman of ideas, he became the victim of his own showman's gift, and he will probably be remembered neither as a playwright nor as a philoso-pher, but chiefly as a man who beat a drum so effectively that he enticed an apathetic public to that main tent where greater men than he were performing.'

The very fact that Shaw's plays are problem plays would indicate that when the problems of our time are no more, so too will his plays be forgotten. With the possible exception of *Saint Joan* there are no great-souled people in Shaw's plays who inspire us to carry their spirit into our lives to make them more beautiful and worthy. His plays start with ideas and problems, not with people. His aim is the dramatization of a problem, not complete presentation of character. His characters attract him by their relationships as members of society rather than as individuals. In this he is typical of his age.

Shaw never tired of comparing himself with Shakespeare, and Shakespeare generally came off worse. Shakespeare was inferior because he had no message for his time. Shaw sent out his first play with the self-assurance of 'If my play *Widowers' Houses* is not better than Shakespear, let it be damned promptly.' One of his publicity stunts was to keep up the comparison, sometimes in not too good taste, as when he spoke about 'people like me and Shakespear'. In the Preface to the *Three Plays for Puritans* he said that *Caesar and Cleopatra* was 'An offer to my public of my Caesar as an improvement on Shakespear's.' Compared with Shakespeare's Caesar and Cleopatra Shaw's seem more like parodies. *Caesar and Cleopatra* is flippant by the side of the intensity of feeling of *Antony and Cleopatra*. Higgins and Eliza have not that sense of universality that informs Shakespeare's figures. Shakespeare lays bare human character, emotions that are eternal – love and hate, joy and sorrow, envy and ambition – great human qualities and little human oddities, in language that is a continual joy to every generation. Shaw's plays present his own views on the problems of his time. Shakespeare said that the stage should 'mirror nature' but it would appear from the Prefaces that Shaw thinks that the stage should *explain* nature. Shaw said (among many other things about the drama), 'A play with a discussion is a modern play. A play with only an emotional situation is an old-fashioned one.'

But Shaw's witty discussion is no substitute for Shakespeare's emotional power. His plays are intellectually keen, crushingly witty, but cynical in tone, without men and women who stir our being. Their appeal is more to the head than to the heart. Whereas Shakespeare could write of mankind, 'What a piece of work is man! how noble in reason! how infinite in faculty! in form and moving how express and admirable! in action how like an angel! in apprehension how like a god! the beauty of the world! the paragon of animals!' Shaw says, 'When I die and go to heaven I shall feel bound in intellectual honour to say to God, "Scrap the lot, Old Man. Your human experiment is a failure. Men as political animals are quite incapable of solving the problems created by the multiplication of their own numbers. Blot them out and make something better!"' With this cynical view of mankind, little wonder that he has made his mark attacking and not enjoying humanity.

Wit, satire and irony abound in his plays, but there is little genial human tolerance. When Shaw laughs he laughs *at* people not *with* them, and his humour leaves a sting. He enjoys wrenching the weaknesses out of human nature more than showing its greatness. He loves to take a stand on his own – paradoxically turning everything inside out, so that what is accepted on all hands as the truth is seen in a very different light. Romantic delusions must be swept away. Whatever is accepted by the general run of mankind Shaw is bound to attack. He likes to be put on his mettle to defend an argument that is hard to defend. Apparently English people like home truths. At any rate by running them down Shaw made a bigger impression on his day and generation than any other of his contemporaries. But, looking to the future, those artists of past ages who are still loved by humanity are those who have themselves had a love of humanity. By no stretch of the imagination can Shaw be said to have this. He examines and overhauls mankind like a garage-hand repairing a car, and then gives it up as a bad job and tells the boss that he had better 'scrap the lot'.

Shaw died on 2 Novermber 1950, as the result of a fall a few months earlier. In Shaw's own Preface to *Pygmalion*, he says that it was his zeal for the reform of the English language that induced him to write a play in which the hero is an 'energetic phonetic enthusiast'. The extent of his interest in the reform of English, or at least English spelling, may be judged from the fact that in his will most of his large fortune was left for a scheme for reforming the English alphabet. (He was man of the world enough, however, to include a clause under which, if this turned out to be impracticable, the money should be divided between the National Gallery of Ireland, the British Museum and the Royal Academy of Dramatic Art.) Six years after his death Shaw's alphabet bequest was declared invalid in the Chancery Court.

It was hoped to raise a great National Memorial Fund in Shaw's honour, to give assistance to causes which would have appealed to him, and also to keep Shaw's Corner, his house at Ayot St Lawrence (where he had lived since 1906) open as a National Memorial. The organizing committee appealed for £250,000; they received £407, and the whole scheme had to be abandoned. This sorry tale makes a bitter commentary on Shaw's confident boasts.

In spite of some decline in his personal popularity in Britain after his death, the interest in his works now seems to be universal, and on the increase.

Plot and themes

Plot

While both are sheltering from a heavy shower of rain Henry Higgins, professor of phonetics, meets a flower-girl with a terrible cockney dialect. He boasts to a bystander that in three months he could train the girl to pass for 'a duchess at an ambassador's party'. The bystander, Colonel Pickering, is interested, for he is an amateur student of Indian dialects, and it turns out that the two men are acquainted with each other's books. Not unnaturally Higgins invites Pickering to visit his laboratory next morning.

During his visit the two men are surprised by a call from the flower-girl, who had overheard their talk the night before. She wants to take lessons in good English, so as to 'be a lady in a flower shop'. Pickering reminds Higgins of his boast and bets him that he cannot carry it out and offers to pay for the experiment. Higgins takes him on, and it is arranged (not without some opposition) that the girl, Eliza Doolittle, shall live at Higgins's house for six months and take the course.

After three months Eliza is tried out at a tea-party given by Higgins's mother. By chance, Mrs Higgins's other guests are the same people who were sheltering from the rain with Eliza in Act 1. In spite of one or two glaring errors – cleverly passed off as the new small talk – Eliza is taken for a lady.

Eventually we learn that Eliza has passed brilliantly as a society lady at a fashionable garden party (though this is not shown on the stage). But at Higgins's rooms after it is over she is bitterly resentful when Higgins can think only of *his own* triumph and considers her merely as a tool in his

hands. He gives her no word of credit for her own determined efforts, without which, she knows, his success would have been impossible. Indeed, he say that 'the whole thing has been simply purgatory' to him – as if it had been pleasant for her!

Next morning she has vanished. In his agitation Higgins calls round at his mother's, only to discover that Eliza has gone there. But she is not the old Eliza. She has a mind of her own and in becoming a lady she has achieved a lady's independence. She refuses to do what Higgins tells her – she will not be 'dirt under his feet'. She thanks Colonel Pickering for his treatment of her; his natural graciousness and courtesy have done most in her real education. But for Higgins, it is quite clear that she will no longer be bound to him, and, in fact, she is glad to be free of him.

Themes

Phonetics

A reader of the Preface and the opening pages of Act 1 could be forgiven for fearing he was embarking on a play about phonetics – such, certainly, is the ostensible theme of *Pygmalion*. But though there is much talk about accents, and the districts where they are spoken, the play soon shows its real concern with more human themes – Shaw was too much of a businessman to base a whole play on a subject of such limited interest as phonetics!

Social class

Class has always been a part of British life – even though today the barriers are less high and the distinctions less marked. And – again peculiarly to Britain – class is a natural follow-on from phonetics: though nowadays an upper-class accent can sometimes be something of a handicap. When Shaw was writing, however, the old standards still dominated – not least those whose social status had improved. When Doolittle informs Eliza that he is going to marry her 'stepmother', she turns on him angrily: 'You're going to let yourself down to marry that low common woman!' (Act 5, p.129). And Higgins (bad-tempered and rude though he can be at times to anyone, of any class) reserves for the flower girl Eliza a brand of offhand scorn he would not dream of showing to a young woman of his own class. (Nevertheless Colonel Pickering's consistent courtesy to Eliza should be noted – good manners are the surest sign of good breeding.)

Shaw's politics

Shaw used all his plays – and other writings – as a more or less overt platform for his Fabian brand of Socialism. He uses *Pygmalion* and the class distinctions, both sharp and subtle, between various characters in the play, to point up the miseries of the lowest members of the working class. We are genuinely moved by Shaw's description of the bedroom Eliza returns to at the end of Act 1 (pp.30–31), after her first meeting with Higgins and the others in the London street where she is selling flowers. However, it is hard to believe that a girl who ultimately displays the spirit and intelligence that Eliza does would be the whining snivelling creature we first meet before Higgins has taken her in hand. And the zest for living and natural ebullience of her father Doolittle seem to 'take over' in the play – against its author's original intentions, we feel.

Compassion

This theme runs through the play, and is directed – openly or by implication – at Eliza. We first find it in Shaw's description of her bedroom, mentioned above. Then, in Act 2, the motherly but brisk and sensible Mrs Pearce, Higgins's housekeeper, exhibits real compassion to the waif she has been commanded to bath, even while calling her a 'foolish ignorant girl' (p.38), 'you silly girl' (p.39), and later 'child'. She remonstrates with Higgins over his attitude to Eliza: 'You must be reasonable, Mr Higgins: really you must. You can't walk over everybody like this' (p.41). She shows Eliza none of the well-known snobbery servants of the time could direct at less fortunate members of their own – or higher – classes.

Higgins's mother shows her concern for Eliza when she discusses the girl's present circumstances and ultimate fate with her son and Colonel Pickering in Act 3 (pp.83–7). When they leave her house, she 'rises with an impatient bounce ... grips the table angrily and exclaims "Oh, men! men!! men!!!"' But the Epilogue makes it clear that both Pickering and Higgins treat Eliza and her husband with kindness and material generosity. Eliza, however, never quite forgives Higgins for his original scorn and near-brutal treatment of her during her 'training' by him.

Eliza's development

Probably the most important theme in the play is Eliza's metamorphosis. Higgins teaches Eliza to speak 'like a lady', and to dress and behave like one. What he hadn't forseen was that her character would also develop until finally she became her own woman. With dignity but resolution she at last puts Higgins and Pickering in their place:

Liza I should like you to call me Eliza, now, if you would.
Pickering Thank you. Eliza, of course.
Liza And I should like Professor Higgins to call me Miss Doolittle.
(Act 5, p.128)

Higgins is delighted at the new spirit she exhibits:

Higgins By George, Eliza, I said I'd make a woman of you; and I have. I like you like this.

Liza Yes: you turn round and make up to me now that I'm not afraid of you, and can do without you. (Act 5,p.138)

Structure and style

Structure

Shaw starts his Preface by saying, 'As will be seen later on, Pygmalion needs, not a preface, but a sequel, which I have supplied in its due place.' Nevertheless he cannot resist writing five pages of unnecessary Preface.

We learn that he became interested in phonetics and the reform of the English language towards the end of the eighteen-seventies. Shaw states that the English spell their language 'so abominably that no man can teach himself what it sounds like.... The reformer England needs to-day is an energetic phonetic enthusiast: that is why I have made such a one the hero of a popular play.' He then pays a tribute to Professor Sweet (Reader in Phonetics at Oxford, and see note on 'Romic' p.54) and says that 'those who knew him will recognize in my third act the allusion to the patent short-hand, in which he used to write postcards. The postcards which Mrs Higgins describes are such as I have received from Sweet.' However, Shaw disclaims all portraiture of Sweet in Professor Higgins.

The Preface is no help in understanding or enjoying the play (though it does give more significance to one or two references mentioned above) and for all practical purposes can be ignored. Were *Pygmalion* about the Science of Phonetics, which is what the Preface implies, it would be in-tolerable.

Act 1 is introductory, showing how the various characters are thrown together, particularly Henry Higgins and Eliza Doolittle.

The action of the play proper starts in Act 2 upon Higgins's acceptance of Pickering's wager. It is continued in

Act 3 when Eliza makes her first appearance in 'society', behaving like a robot, until she forgets herself and lets herself go. Even then her mistakes are covered up.

But when Act 4 opens her triumph is all over. In the two following acts we see first of all how rebellion simmers in Eliza as she comes to realize that she has been used as a guinea-pig and that her trainers have no further use for her, and secondly how her indignation bursts out and sets her soul free.

It has been said that the play is badly constructed because what ought to be the climax – the success of Eliza at the garden party or the dinner party – is left out, so far as the stage is concerned. But this is a bookish point of view. At the garden party Eliza behaves perfectly: such a scene would be without the uproarious laughter which always greets her incongruous remarks in Act 3. To have both scenes on the stage would, of course, be unthinkable, the second would prove merely a wearisome anti-climax.

In her *Memoirs* Mrs Patrick Campbell, who took the part of Eliza in all the London performances up to 1920, said of *Pygmalion*, 'The last act of the play did not travel across the footlights with as clear dramatic sequence as the preceding acts – owing entirely to the fault of the writer.' It is natural, perhaps, that a famous actress should blame the author for any failure in the theatre. Might it not be that in her presentation the great actress mistook the climax of the play, as a number of critics have done? Shaw surely did not intend to place his climax off-stage between Acts 3 and 4, and then bore his audience with two superfluous acts to fill up the time. The climax is in Act 5, where Eliza becomes a person in her own right – 'If I cant have kindness, I'll have independence': where she shows that she can stand on her own feet, without Higgins to lean upon (as in Act 3) 'I'm not afraid of you, and can do without you.' At the end of the play she tells

Higgins that she will not be seeing him again. She will be an unpaid servant no longer, and he can get along as best he can.

In Acts 2 and 3 Eliza is made a mechanical lady; in Acts 4 and 5, leading on from that, she *becomes* (the distinction is significant) a live woman. Many of Shaw's chief characters undergo complete transformation: Eliza Doolittle is twice transformed. The tables are turned on Higgins: in Act 1 Higgins despises Eliza – indeed he makes no attempts to hide his feelings about her; in Act 5 it is Eliza's turn to despise Higgins, and she likewise does not fail to tell him so.

This is where the significance of the title becomes evident. Pygmalion made a statue that came alive: Eliza can hardly be said to be fully alive at the garden party or at the opera; she was acting to a set pattern. But in Act 5 she became a lady with a heart and soul, a personality in her own right. 'By George, Eliza, I said I'd make a woman of you; and I have.'

Thus Eliza's outlook is changed as well as her language; in the construction of the play the two correspond, though they are not concurrent. Briefly, there is an inner change as well as an outer change. It is going too far to say that her *character* is changed; it is truer to say that it had been repressed during her tutelage.

The Eynsford Hills, of course, are merely incidental, a control group to throw up the deviations of Eliza from the norm.

Parallel to Eliza's own exaltation, her father Alfred Doolittle is unexpectedly lifted out of the slums. But his fortune is an accident; he has had no part in it. (Incidentally, the contrivance in the plot by which he is brought into money sounds rather far-fetched.) And it means a change in position only: there is (for all he says) no change in mind and outlook. He is too old for that. Rich or poor he is 'undeserving' still. Thus a parallel interest is given diversity and is prevented from being merely a repeat of the main plot. Alfred Doolittle represents the opposite plane of morality to the conventional one represented by Higgins and Pickering. Father and daughter alike come to value independence and personal freedom above mere fortune.

The play is constructed so as to make the most of contrast on the stage – between the comfortably off and the desperately poor, the strict and the dissolute, the polite man of the world and the boorish specialist – to say nothing of the old and the new Eliza.

In the Epilogue, having determined that Higgins is not the right man for her, Eliza opts to marry Freddy whose love for her is undeniable. Complications ensue: but they are economic rather than romantic. With some financial help from the Colonel, they open a flower shop in the arcade of a railway station not very far from the Victoria and Albert Museum probably South Kensington station). The young couple work very hard and take evening classes in short-hand, bookkeeping and typewriting. Slowly but surely, the deficit made up annually by the Colonel disappears and the business prospers.

Meanwhile, Freddy's sister Clara is also given a new lease of life. Two events cause her to lose her snobbery overnight: the first is her astonishment at learning that the young woman whom she so admired had, but three months hence, risen from the gutter and the second is her conversion to the works of H. G. Wells. She further astounds her family by announcing that she is going to work in a furniture shop in Dover Street, started by a fellow Wellsian.

Style

It has been said that *Pygmalion* is Shaw's most characteristic play. This is true of its style too. There is indeed little sense of grace, form and choice in Shaw's style. Like many modern authors he is not concerned with techniques of style, and he does not yearn after fine writing. His style has an intellectual quality of the first order: it is a model of clarity. But it lacks beauty: it is clear but cold. One could do with more warmth of feeling, more heart and less head. It was the matter rather than the manner of Shaw's plays that set people astir at the turn of the century.

The speeches of many of Shaw's characters are like public orations; they give the effect not of a fireside talk but of an official debate. Doolittle's speeches are much too long and philosophical, and their vocabulary too difficult for a dustman. Shaw uses him to press home his paradoxical arguments. It is not uncommon for Shaw's dramatis personae to be more intelligent and witty than they would be in real life; they speak as if they have Bernard Shaw's head on their own bodies. Ordinary people do not sit down to explain their philosophy of life in long speeches. Their philosophy of life is implicit in their words and actions, and so should it be in a play. Doolittle's words do not fit his character; the material and the style of his longer speeches make him into a ventriloquist's dummy, in very truth a 'live doll', to use a term applied to his daughter. It should be noted, however, that though Doolittle's long speeches are thoughtful and his arguments unexpected in their conclusions, the sentences are short making the gist easier to follow and the speeches more dramatic.

The Americanized spelling of the play (e.g. splendor, favor, parlor-maid) and the omission of the apostrophe ('e' too, at times): wont, havnt, arnt, are arbitrary tricks of style and do not affect its texture. Incidentally Shaw shows how he was on his own ground in this play – he had his own ideas on the representation of English sounds, and being a famous author whose work was in demand could indulge them. He usually allows the apostrophe *s* to show a possessive, e.g. Higgins's, but his use to show a shortening of *is* is irregular, and we have 'he's' and 'who's hurting', but 'wheres' and 'theres' and 'thats what he is'.

Shaw writes with his eye on the stage. He sees every detail in the scenery and props, and leaves nothing to chance. In this connection the student should consider especially the stage directions to Acts 2 and 3. In Act 2 the time is *11 a.m.* (not just 'in the morning') in *Higgins's laboratory in Wimpole Street*, and not only the furniture but all the odds and ends about the room are described in detail. And so throughout, until in the last act we are told when Higgins sits in the Elizabethan chair and when in the Chippendale, a detail which most playwrights would leave to the producer.

Corresponding attention to detail is to be found in the exact location of scenes in the play, e.g. under the portico of St Paul's Church, 27A Wimpole Street, a flat on Chelsea Embankment. Here the linking of fictitious events with actual places makes the fiction seem more real. The events of *Pygmalion* happen in a small clearly defined locality. Most of the places mentioned are well known to Londoners, and the place-names to many who live far from London (e.g. Covent Garden), and their existence corroborates the truth of the play as it were. These actual place-names are a powerful aid in giving the illusion of reality.

Similarly Shaw sees his characters in detail and describes them at length, as, for instance, in the description of Higgins in the extended stage directions to Act 2. There are touches of detail which most dramatists would consider superfluous in many of the shorter directions, for example when Eliza enters a little later in Act 2 we are told that, '*she has a hat with three ostrich feathers, orange, sky-blue, and red.*'

In addition to a description of the appearance of his dramatis personae, Shaw not infrequently sketches their character in some detail. Such is the description of Higgins in the last paragraph of the stage direction opening Act 2. By doing this the dramatist dictates what we should think about his characters before we see them in action or hear their words. Half the joy of seeing (or reading) a play is to speculate on the characters and to see what life means to them from their words, actions and influence in the play. The dramatist who provides us with his official version of their characters takes away that pleasure and, incidentally, makes his work less dramatic. The play thus gives the impression of being half play, half novel, much like radio dramatizations. This may help the reader, but is certainly superfluous in a stage production. It is further indication of how Shaw wrote his plays to be read as much as to be acted.

The student will notice that in Act 1 (except for Freddy) the characters are referred to by the part they are taking instead of by name, and their names are not supplied until after they have been introduced to one another in the play. This is dramatic. When a character first appears, he has no claim to the interest of the audience, he has to make it. Just as the other characters in the play have to find out his name so does the spectator (or reader) of the play.

The wit, humour and irony which are the essence of Shaw's writing need no illustration. The student will find them everywhere. Such never-to-be-forgotten remarks as, 'I dont want to talk grammar. I want to talk like a lady': or the humour (and underlying pathos) of

Higgins Somebody is going to touch you, with a broomstick, if you dont stop snivelling. Sit down.

Liza [*obeying slowly*] Ah-ah-ah-ow-oo-o! One would think you was my father.

or the paradox of 'Time enough to think of the future when you havnt any future to think of': or the irony of Eliza's ill-bred shriek just after she has said, 'I have learnt my lesson. I dont believe I could utter one of the old sounds if I tried.' Apart from repartee in dialogue the humour attributable to Eliza's appearances is, of course, humour of situation rather than of character.

Characters

Higgins

'Youve no feeling heart in you: you dont care for nothing but yourself.'

The appearance and character of Higgins are sketched briefly for us in the stage directions to Act 2, and the dramatist remarks on several other qualities of his character in the course of the Act.

Henry Higgins, a professor of phonetics, who earns his living teaching *parvenus* good English, is a narrow-minded, strong-willed man of nearly forty. He lives only for his work. Whenever he talks about it he speaks heartily and with enthusiasm. It was his boast concerning his talent in phonetics that brought him the tuition of Eliza. He did not take on the bet out of pity for a poor girl, to try and improve her, but to show what he could do, 'because it was my job'. He does his work thoroughly and ably, but without consideration for the girl's feelings. He walks over everybody, as Mrs Pearce says, including his mother's guests, so much so that she has earnestly requested him not to visit her on her at-home days. 'You offend all my friends: they stop coming whenever they meet you.'

When Eliza is a visitor, a rather timid visitor, at his home, he disposes of her so roughly that she runs between Pickering and Mrs Pearce for protection. But his temper calms down as quickly as it is roused: 'The hurricane is succeeded by a zephyr of amiable surprise.' It was like this in the portico of St Paul's Church. One minute he was slandering Eliza, calling her a liar, the next he was showering a handful of coins into her basket, a creature of impulse, rude even in his

R.money.

generosity. He gets 'in a state' four or five times in the play – most of all when Eliza threatens to run off to one of his competitors with the secrets of his art. This is the man who had said that he had hardly ever lost his temper. He is so self-centred that he cannot see how anyone could be offended by his words or his manner, and he makes a silly excuse which convinces no one except himself – 'If I did not express myself clearly it was because I did not wish to hurt her delicacy, or yours.' Similarly he emphatically protests that he never swears and uses a borderline expression in saying so. When Pickering and he are shouting one another down to make Mrs Higgins appreciate Eliza's virtues, Pickering apologizes, but Higgins blames Pickering – 'When Pickering starts shouting nobody can get a word in edgeways.' The blame must always be put somewhere else. He fails to see the beam in his own eye for the mote in another's.

Similarly Higgins magnifies other people's misdeeds – 'She threw my slippers in my face. She behaved in the most outrageous way. I never gave her the slightest provocation. The slippers came bang into my face the moment I entered the room – before I had uttered a word. And used perfectly awful language.' The student has only to turn back a page or two to see how grossly this is exaggerated. When Mrs Higgins says Eliza shall come down 'If you promise to behave yourself, Henry,' Henry agrees as if the condition applied to Pickering – 'Very well, Pick: you behave yourself.' There can be no wrong in *him*. People like this are generally susceptible to flattery and Higgins is no exception. When there is no one else to sing his praises he fills in the gap himself. He is full of himself, and oozes with self-assurance. He is very thick-skinned, and very clever in twisting circumstances to accuse others and exonerate himself. He will never alter – 'incorrigible' is Shaw's word for him, as, at the end, he resists Eliza's disdain and in a 'cheerful, careless, vigorous voice' gives her his shopping order.

Higgins admits to Pickering that it never occurred to him that Eliza had any feelings, and 'when I've done with her,' he says, 'we can throw her back into the gutter'. As Mrs Pearce says, 'When you get what you call interested in people's accents, you never think or care what may happen to them or you.' People who are not likely to fall in with his views he condemns as blackguards before he has seen them (Alfred Doolittle), yet he swears that he is 'a shy, diffident sort of man'. Higgins wants to talk down everybody else. At one point Pickering has to plead with him to let Alfred Doolittle tell his story. He is 'all bounce and go, and no consideration for anyone.' IMPETUOUS BABY

The person who can manage this 'confirmed old bachelor' best is, not surprisingly, his mother. She humours him suavely and treats him half as a boy, as mothers commonly do their grown-up sons. But even she, after pleading and reproof, cannot make him behave politely to her visitors. He thinks only of himself and he always says what he thinks without pausing to consider other people's feelings. Before her at-home visitors he is bluntly outspoken, and it is obvious why his mother wants him out of the way on such occasions. There is little evidence that he loves his mother. In the course of the play he does little for her. He perhaps loves her from habit, but not from a considered loyalty.

Higgins's table manners leave much to be desired but Mrs Pearce is not slow to draw his attention to this (Act 2). However, in all probability, his manners are no worse than the majority of people living on their own. Those who live with only one absorbing interest are often difficult to get on with. Higgins has led a sheltered life, never mixing much with his fellows, standing behind pillars writing notes about them instead. He divides men up into Lisson Grove or Epsom or Cheltenham, and judges them accordingly. Since his own speech is so much better than the average, and speech is the only thing that matters in life, he is self-opinionated, and treats other people boorishly. As we have said, he undertook to improve Eliza's speech not for *her* sake but for his own – to show how much he could do with unpromising material. When he has done it his lack of sympathy for other people (even the girl who had been his daily pupil) is seen only too shamefully. Eliza has tried really hard, but he has never noticed that. He blindly imagines that all her success is due to the teacher. 'You won my bet! You! Presumptuous insect! *I* won it.' He has done the job he was engaged to do, and now he tells her that she has served her purpose and he has lost interest in her. Eliza realizes that she counts for nothing and that she has been looked upon as a mere tool, and she runs off in desperation. Then the chief thing that seems to annoy Higgins is that he has lost a cheap servant – 'I cant find anything. I dont know what appointments Ive got. I'm—.' All the time *I, I, I,* – never does it occur to him that *she* may be miserable or in danger. Experts, at the top in their own narrow field, get an unbalanced view of life, and think that their pet subject is the only thing that matters. They get narrower and narrower in outlook as they get deeper and deeper in their own narrow groove. Higgins's soul has been slowly deadened, whereas Eliza's is suddenly brought to life.

The kindest view to take of Higgins is that he is a great artist, whose art impells him to ignore every other consideration. He was certainly expert at his work. Pickering thought that he had given him an impossible task to perform, but when the six months is over he has to admit that Eliza has been a great success and the occasion a triumph for Higgins. And if Higgins is outspoken to the point of rudeness, let it be remembered that he is not a snob; he is rude to *everyone*, irrespective of class: he is not, for instance, polite to Mrs Eynsford Hill and rude to the parlour maid, he is rude all round.

Ironically enough it is through his success in educating Eliza that at the end of the play the modern Pygmalion is pushed down from his pedestal to take second place to her. He has not only taught her correct language, he has (unintentionally) given her something to live for, and a dynamic personality of her own. At the beginning of the play he is the more masterful figure; at the end, she is.   ← IRONY   ⑬

Eliza

'Ive won your bet for you, havnt I?'

Eliza is the central figure of the play – 'heroine' would be the wrong word. The circumstances in which she is placed give her more interest than her character as such.

This creature of the slums, an outcast from birth, shabby and filthy (though Shaw makes the point that she is as clean as she can afford to be), whose incomprehensible cockney dialect betrays her origin in every word, yearns after higher things; when the opportunity comes her way she grasps it and calls on Higgins for lessons in proper speech. To do this shows initiative and determination. Everyone is against her, and even those who buy flowers do so from pity. Eliza has never known a home, is one of those dragged up not brought up. She has never found anyone who wanted her (not even her father), nor anyone to whom she meant anything. When she meets someone who needs her and at the same time will provide comparative luxury, it is hardly surprising that her first opposition, the result of an instinctive suspicion, soon breaks down. True, she is wanted only for an experiment, but still, the experiment, if successful, will enable her to

'talk like a lady' and sell flowers in a proper flower shop
– the height of her ambition. At first she 'dont want no
balmies' teaching her, but nice frocks and tasty chocolates
prove an attraction she cannot resist. None the less she
must be determined by nature to have suffered the humilia-
tion and insults which Higgins heaps upon her, notwith-
standing fashionable clothes and 'barrels' of chocolates every
day.

But the newly rich poor girl is the biggest snob of all and
the first thing she wants to do in her new life is to go and
show off, 'put the girls in their places a bit'. Eliza's sudden
advancement has gone to her head. She judges her former
associates by their postion, not by their personality. They are
beneath her now. She does not fill her new position as if she
was *used to it*.

By the time of Mrs Higgins's at-home Eliza has learnt a
new language, and 'exquisitely dressed' she 'produces an
impression of such remarkable distinction and beauty as
she enters that they all rise, quite fluttered. Guided by
Higgins's signals, she comes to Mrs Higgins with studied
grace.' This was the very girl whom Mrs Eynsford Hill
pitied in Act 1. Her dress and her talk get her over the first
hurdle – though not without difficulty, for she is a congenial
soul, not slow of tongue, and, after a correct but stiff
beginning, she is soon the centre of the party when she gets
off her prepared subjects and drops into her vernacular. This
part of the play gets the biggest roars of laughter on the
stage, and (by a stretch of the imagination, it must be
admitted) Eliza's mistakes get by as 'the new small talk'.

One might imagine that on the night of her 'immense
success' she would be very happy. But Eliza is more miserable then than ever before. She has responded, and done her
best, and not once has she received a word of praise. The
acquiring of good English must have been exceptionally

difficult for Eliza. Yet she has exceeded what her tutor thought possible. She feels now that she is something to some-body, that someone has faith in her. The blow comes when 'they take no notice of her'. Her efforts go for nothing. Higgins can talk only of *his own* success. She does not count. 'You dont care ... I'm nothing to you – not so much as them slippers.' She is a nonentity, an instrument that has been tested, yielded certain results and can now be got rid of.

This is a shock to Eliza: she has worked hard to succeed. She is no fool; she has plenty of natural ability (she quickly learns to play the piano well by ear). She has tried not just for herself but 'because we were pleasant together and I come – came – to care for you; not to want you to make love to me, and not forgetting the difference between us, but more friendly like.' It was a new experience to have somebody who cared for her (even if only as a subject for experiment) and her heart warmed to it. Henry and the Colonel were the only people who had ever done anything for her – whatever their purpose – 'I have no real friends in the world but you and the Colonel.'

In submitting herself in docile fashion to Higgins's instruc-tion Eliza had acted unnaturally for a far purpose, her real self had been repressed. Now nobody wants her. It is all a dream. She is back where she was. Higgins treats her like his property, like a curio in his collection. It is this that gives strength to her arm as she throws his slippers in his face. In desperation she runs off and in rebelling, regains her inde-pendence. 'If I cant have kindness, I'll have independence.' 'Why did you take my independence from me?' 'Why did I give it up? I'm a slave now, for all my fine clothes.' When Eliza was a flower girl she provided for herself and owed no man anything. Now she owes her success to other people. She values her independence: it is a great thing in life. She valued it as a flower-girl and provided herself with an honest

living as a 'good girl' when worse courses were open to her. She 'only wants to be natural'. But being natural now, after mixing for six months with a different set, means something different. The basis is, however, the same; the careful habits of a flower girl persist, and after Higgins's exit she searches carefully for the ring he had thrown into the fireplace. Incidentally this shows how well she can act a part. She was deliberately inciting Higgins. She knows what she wants quite well.

Higgins had taught Eliza only the mechanics, the formalities of etiquette. He may know all about speech but he knows nothing of human nature. He has no understanding. Furthermore, he is too rude himself to be qualified to teach her good manners. It was from Colonel Pickering that Eliza absorbed the essence of the ease and graciousness of good manners without being taught, and she herself realizes it. It was when she *was treated* as a lady that most was done to make her one. It was Pickering who asked her courteously if she would not sit down (when Higgins could only bully her), and it was he who called her Miss Doolittle (the first time ever that she had been so addressed, apparently).

Do you know what began my real education? ... Your calling me Miss Doolittle that day when I first came to Wimpole Street. That was the beginning of self-respect for me. And there were a hundred little things you never noticed, because they came naturally to you. ... Things that shewed you thought and felt about me as if I were something better than a scullery-maid; though of course I know you would have been just the same to a scullery-maid if she had been let into the drawing room.

Practice was of more importance than precept.

In the end, Eliza regains her soul, and her independence is the greatest thing in life; she states her own terms for remaining with Higgins, and when they are not accepted she

bids him goodbye. She now has a will of her own. Higgins
gave her the outward trappings of a lady, now she becomes
one in her own right. Higgins himself recognizes it— 'By
George, Eliza, I said I'd make a woman of you; and I have.'
It is interesting to speculate on what would have been the end
of the play if Higgins had thanked Eliza for her efforts and
treated her as a human being.

Shaw pooh poohs romance, yet cannot resist a happy
ending by means of the most unlikely coincidences. By a
freak chance her dustman father becomes rich; a husband is
found for her; and in the epilogue, at all events, she is spoken
of as wife and mother. This sort of ending is more like
Dickens than Shaw. Shaw's explanation of Eliza's preference
of Freddie to Higgins (even supposing Higgins were the
marrying sort) is quite unnecessary. It was the only choice.

Doolittle

'I'm one of the undeserving poor: thats what I am.'

When *Pygmalion* was first produced in London, Mr Desmond
MacCarthy wrote in *The New Statesman and Nation* that
'Mr Doolittle (so admirably played by Mr Gurney) is Mr
Shaw's most amusing achievement' and there is no doubt
that he makes a lasting impression. Eliza and her father rank
among the best characters in modern comedy.

Doolittle was introduced into the play for the fun of the
thing, and is not in character as a dustman. Who ever
heard of a dustman being disappointed at coming into £3,000
a year? In theory his reasons are sound enough, but they
are the reasons of a playwright, not those of a dustman who
up to now has lived on thirty shillings (£1.50) a week.
Money, finds this articulate dustman, does not compensate
him for the loss of the freedom he enjoyed as a poor man.
The thought that happiness cannot exist without freedom

and independence comes to Eliza as well and gives a unity to the thought of the play.

Doolittle is a mouthpiece for Shaw's paradoxes; for example, that a woman is better off living unwed with a man than as his lawful wife – 'I'm a slave to that woman, Governor, just because I'm not her lawful husband. And she knows it too. Catch her marrying me!' Shaw is never happier than when he is ridiculing conventional beliefs.

The philosophic dustman is overdone in the spirit of Dickensian caricature. It is not even barely credible, let alone convincing, that a dustman with this piece of good fortune would say, 'I ... have nothing between me and the pauper's uniform but this here blasted three thousand a year that shoves me into the middle class.' He comes to Higgins 'with vehement reproach' and, overcome by emotion, he denounces her son before Mrs Higgins as the agent of his ill luck.

His 'ticket' name labels his character and makes us realize that he is incurably lazy, and like all of us he has thought out good reasons for living the kind of life he prefers. Shaw uses a name instead of a longer description to explain his character. (It is not an imaginary name, however. The name Doolittle is found in the West Midlands, particularly near Kidderminster.) Doolittle has completely shirked his responsibilities. He has been content to let his illegitimate child shift for herself, hungry and in rags and squalor, until she is old enough to look after herself, at which point he turns her out. 'I aint got no parents. They told me I was big enough to earn my own living and turned me out.' He shows no interest in her and cares nothing what happens to her. He comes to Higgins quickly enough to get £5 for her, but his interest ends there and he is quite unconcerned about her welfare in Higgins's hands.

This dustman-cum-pickpocket is a most improbable

character who makes a memorable impression on the stage because of his clever arguments and original philosophy put over in brilliantly witty speeches. As Pickering says in another connection, 'Very clever, Higgins: but not sound sense.'

Colonel Pickering

Higgins and Pickering first strike up a friendship as a result of their consuming interest in phonetics; the similarity, however, ends there. Higgins is the archetypal confirmed bachelor to whom social niceties are of little importance; Pickering is the perfect gentleman (indeed this is how Shaw first introduces him to the audience in Act 1). He is always respectful in his dealings with others: in the first act, Pickering apologizes twice to the flower-girl as he has no change with which to buy her flowers. He is also courteous and throughout the play, addresses Eliza as Miss Doolittle.

Having goaded Higgins into accepting the challenge of transforming Eliza into a lady, Pickering readily accepts the responsibility for her moral welfare. As his friendship with the Professor is of short standing Pickering asks him, 'Are you a man of good character where women are concerned?' He accepts Higgins's gentleman's word on this score and later we see him defending Higgins: 'Higgins' intentions are entirely honourable'.

During Eliza's elocution lessons, we see Pickering cast in the role of mediator between pupil and teacher 'Do what he tells you and let him teach you in his own way.' He recognizes the need for encouragement 'Good. Splendid, Miss Doolittle', and it is probable that Eliza's transformation could not have taken place without Pickering's help. Indeed, Eliza acknowledges this in the final act 'And I should never have known that ladies and gentleman didn't behave like that if you hadnt been there.'

Minor characters

Mrs Higgins

Mrs Higgins knows her son only too well and indeed she is is the only character in the play who can be said fully to understand the Professor. Her patience has obviously been tried by her son's intolerable behaviour – she has had to ban him from her 'at-home' days as he has succeeded in offending most of her friends. Though in his forties, Mrs Higgins still has to remind her son to remove his hat when he enters her home; and it soon becomes clear from their conversation that she treats him like an overgrown baby: 'Stop fidgeting and take your hands out of your pockets.' The 'at-home' lives up to Mrs Higgins's worst expectations; and once her guests have departed, she demands an explanation of her son's intentions *vis-à-vis* Eliza's future. When both Higgins and Pickering admit to never having given this a thought, Mrs Higgins cries out, 'Oh, men! men!! men!!!' Her common sense and consideration of others would not have allowed her to enter into an experiment such as this without due consideration of the flower girl's future.

When Eliza runs away from Wimpole Street, she seeks refuge with the only person who has treated her well over the six-month period – Mrs Higgins. She in turn is quick to take her son to task over his brutal treatment of the girl: 'You didnt thank her or pet her, or admire her, or tell her how splendid shed been.' She is also concerned enough about Eliza's welfare to ask Doolittle to step out on to the balcony, and wait until Eliza has made her peace with Pickering and Higgins, before surprising her with his piece of news.

In all, Mrs Higgins displays all the proper maternal qualities and enjoys none of the benefits of filial love.

The Eynsford Hill family

The only members of this family that we meet are Mrs
Eynsford Hill and her two children Freddy and Clara, both
of whom are in awe of their domineering mother; Freddy in
particular suffers both his mother's and his sister's remon-
strances. Freddy and Clara are easily led and quickly
transfer their admiration to Eliza: Freddy falls helplessly
in love with her from the moment he casts eyes on her at
Mrs Higgins's 'at-home'; and Clara, eager to be considered
thoroughly up to date, imitates all that Eliza does. Mrs
Eynsford Hill can only look on aghast.

These characters are only roughly sketched in by Shaw as
their sole purpose is to highlight Eliza's changing lifestyle and
to throw up her deviations from what was regarded as the
norm (as represented by the Evnsford Hills).

Act summaries, textual notes
and revision questions

Act 1

In a sudden heavy storm at 11.15 one summer night, pedestrians run for shelter under the portico of St Paul's Church in Covent Garden, where a lady and her daughter in evening dress and a man writing in a notebook have already gathered. The two ladies have evidently been to the Royal Opera House or a theatre and are annoyed with Freddy, the lady's son, who has been unable to find a cab. Freddy now rushes in out of the rain declaring that there is not a cab to be had for love or money. Mother and Daughter are very unsympathetic, refuse to listen to his excuses and send him off again. As he dashes off he bumps into a flower girl, and sends her basket flying. The girl complains (in 'kerbstone' English) and Freddy's mother pays for the damaged blooms – much against the wish of her daughter. The Flower Girl tries to follow this up with a sale to a gentleman standing by.

The Flower Girl is now warned by another Bystander to be careful what she is doing, as 'theres a bloke here behind taking down every blessed word youre saying.' She becomes hysterical and this starts a hubbub. The Note Taker comforts her briefly, says he is not a policeman and astounds them all by correctly locating the place where they come from as soon as they speak. They are so absorbed that they fail to notice the rain has stopped until this is pointed out by the Note Taker. Thereupon people walk off, Mother and Daughter hurrying to catch a bus, all except the Note Taker, the Gentleman and the Flower Girl. The Gentleman shows great interest in the Note Taker's performance and asks him how he does it. Simply by phonetics, he is told.

It turns out that the Gentleman is Colonel Pickering, an expert on Indian dialects and the author of *Spoken Sanscrit*. He has come from India specially to meet the Note Taker, Henry Higgins, author of *Higgins's Universal Alphabet*. They greet one another with enthusiasm and arrange to have supper together; Higgins invites Pickering to come and see him the following day. As he goes Higgins 'throws a handful of money' into the Flower Girl's basket.

Just then Freddy springs out of a taxicab he has at last managed to get and finds out from the Flower Girl that his mother and sister have set off to walk to the bus. 'And left me with a cab on my hands! Damnation!' he bursts out. 'Never mind, young man. *I'm* going home in a taxi,' is the startling reply. And so she does, telling the driver to see 'how fast you can make her hop it'.

Pygmalion In Classical mythology Pygmalion (of the play's title) was a sculptor who carved a statue of a woman in ivory and prayed to Venus to breathe life into it. The goddess answered his prayer (and he married his living statue). In the Epilogue Higgins is said to be Eliza's Pygmalion.

Covent Garden In the centre of London's theatreland – see map p.5. (So named after the Convent Garden of Westminster, which stood on the site.) Famous once as the site of the Covent Garden vegetable market.

Cab whistles i.e. whistles of people who wanted cabs.

portico covered walk – on the East End (not the entrance to the Church, which is on the West End).

St Paul's Church The Church built by Inigo Jones in 1633 (not to be confused with St Paul's Cathedral). The student will see from the map (p.5) that Inigo Place leads up to it. After its destruction by fire in 1795 the church was rebuilt according to the original design of Inigo Jones. In the church there is a casket containing the ashes of Ellen Terry (d. 1928), a great friend of Bernard Shaw.

gumption common sense (colloquial).

Ludgate Circus A mile away from St Paul's Church.

Hammersmith A west London borough, some seven miles away.

wh' y' gowin Where are you going?

eez ... them? He's your son, is he? Well, if you had done your duty by him as a mother should, he would know better than to spoil a poor girl's flowers and then run away without paying. Will you pay me for them?

a tanner Sixpence (slang).

Garn Corruption of 'go on'.

hollerin Shouting out (slang).

copper's nark Police spy (slang). The Bystander has learnt how to tell anyone in the police force by his boots.

Selsey A small seaside resort in West Sussex (just west of Selsey Bill) and some eight miles south of Chichester.

Park Lane One of the most fashionable streets in London, facing Hyde Park (see map p.4).

Housing Question Our present-day Housing Question is nothing new. There always has been a Housing Problem in this country, at least since the Industrial Revolution.

Hoxton A small London suburb, a mile or so east of King's Cross Station, but not real East End.

Bly me! A mild oath, corresponding to 'Good gracious!' though literally a corruption of 'God blind me'.

no truck Any dealings.

Cheltenham, Harrow, Cambridge, and India The Note Taker is probably going through the situation of his preparatory school, public school, university and career. In those days many university men made their career in the Indian army or in administrative posts in India. Cheltenham, in Gloucestershire, was an important educational centre of private schools; Harrow, of course, refers to the famous public school just north-west of London, and Cambridge to Cambridge University.

music hall A place of light entertainment, very popular in the days before the cinema.

Earlscourt (Earl's Court); part of West Kensington.

Epsom A Surrey town sixteen miles from Covent Garden in a south-south-westerly direction.

produces a whistle See note on 'Cab whistles' above.

Hanwell A suburb adjoining Ealing – on the west side.

motor bus Notice the qualifying adjective in 1912. Horse buses were running on the London streets as late as 1904.

gathers her skirts above her ankles In Edwardian days ladies wore ankle-length skirts, indeed until the First World War.

worrited Vulgarism for 'worried'.

Irishman Shaw himself was an Irishman who had come to London (see *The author and his work*).

Yorkshireman Yorkshire occupies a large area of the North of England (it is England's largest county) and there are always plenty of Yorkshire folk in London.

Kentish Town At that time a slum area of London, north of Camden Town – the opposite of Park Lane (see note above).

boohooing Noisy crying.

place of worship Sarcastically said, i.e. not a place for 'boohooing'.

Shakespear England's greatest dramatist (1564–1616). This is Shaw's spelling.

Milton England's greatest epic poet (1608–74).

better English i.e. than that of a Duchess. (More sarcasm.)

Sanscrit The ancient and sacred language of India.

the Carlton i.e. the Carlton Hotel (no longer in existence).

jaw Chat (slang).

Pharisaic Self-righteous, hypocritical, like the Pharisees of the Gospels.

half-sovereign A gold coin until 1914.

Angel Court An imaginary place. For 'Drury Lane' see maps.

Revision Questions on Act 1

1 Describe the scene under the portico of St Paul's Church, Covent Garden, at 11.15 p.m. on the night the play opens.

2 Describe how the Flower Girl is brought into conversation with the Mother and her Daughter.

3 How does it happen that the Note Taker creates a stir among the people taking shelter?

4 Give examples of the Note Taker's accuracy in telling people where they came from.

5 Why do the Note Taker and the Gentleman suddenly strike up a friendship?

6 Describe how the Flower Girl leaves the stage at the end of the scene.

Act 2

Next morning Pickering duly pays his visit to Higgins's laboratory and when the scene opens has just seen 'the whole show' (of his instruments for recording speech). Then the housekeeper announces the arrival of a young woman, and the Flower Girl is brought in. At first Higgins wants to send her off (she had passed completely from his mind), but the Flower Girl tells him that she has come to bring him business: she wants to take elocution lessons so that she can 'be a lady in a flower shop stead of selling at the corner of Tottenham Court Road'. She will pay for her lessons out of the money Higgins 'chucked at her' the night before. She offers one shilling per lesson, which impresses Higgins as an enormous sum in terms of her income. Pickering reminds him of his boast of the night before that in three months he 'could pass that girl off as a duchess at an ambassador's garden party'. He calls Higgins's bluff and offers to cover the costs of the experiment; he will also pay for the lessons. Higgins accepts the challenge. First of all he tells his house-keeper that the girl must be cleaned up, her old clothes burned and some new clothes bought. There is much fun over the girl's misapprehension of his intentions. However, in the end she agrees to stay and be a guinea-pig; Eliza has been won over by promises of 'chocolates, and taxis, and gold, and diamonds'. Mrs Pearce, the housekeeper, bundles her off to the bathroom. Before long Mrs Pearce comes back to ask Higgins to be careful of his language in front of the girl, especially as regards one word, which she has heard the girl use in the bathroom; she also takes this opportunity to correct some of Higgins's other bad habits.

Meanwhile Alfred Doolittle, the father of the girl, has arrived on Higgins's doorstep asking after Eliza. It appears that he does not want her back, he simply wants to 'touch' Higgins for £5 on the strength of his keeping Eliza. He is indifferent to what happens to her, and Eliza for her part 'never wants to see him again'. Meeting his daughter at the door, clean and daintily dressed in a Japanese outfit, as he is hurrying out 'with his booty', he fails to recognize her until she speaks to him.

The scene ends with Eliza asking for a taxi to go to Tottenham Court Road 'just to put the girls in their place a bit', and 'get a bit of her own back'. At Pickering's suggestion she puts off the idea until she has some really fashionable clothes to go in. At this point Mrs Pearce comes back to tell Eliza that her new clothes have come and Eliza rushes out to see them with a whoop of delight.

Higgins and Pickering realize that they have 'taken on a stiff job'.

phonograph An instrument automatically recording and reproducing sounds, working on the principle of the gramophone; an old-fashioned instrument doing the work of a modern tape-recorder. It looked like the gramophone in the *His Master's Voice* trade mark.

laryngoscope A mirror apparatus for examining the larynx.

Piranesis The work of Piranesi, an Italian engraver using copper plates, who was called the 'Rembrandt of Architecture' (1720–78). Most of his engravings show the splendours of ancient Rome still preserved in the Rome of his own day. His claim to immortality rests on his etchings.

mezzotint Reproduced by a method of tone engraving.

Bell's Visible Speech The subsidiary title of this book (published 1867) gave its purpose – ' The Science of Universal Alphabetics or Self-Interpreting Physiological Letters for the writing of All Languages in one Alphabet'. It was an expensive book, 75p for 142 quarto pages – a lot of money in those days. The author, Alexander Melville Bell, called himself a Professor of Vocal Physiology and was Lecturer in Elocution in University College, London. He was a man very much like Higgins, and his terms for private lessons in speech were one guinea for a single lesson or three guineas for six lessons. A page of his 'Visible Speech' looks like so much Chinese to the uninitiated.

Romic A system of phonetics devised by Dr H. Sweet. It is explained in his *Handbook of Phonetics*, so named, he says, 'because based on the original Roman values of the letters'.

feather-weight cross i.e. light (imaginary) burden, the cross being a metaphor from the Cross of Christ. The meaning comes out in the next stage direction, where Higgins makes 'an intolerable grievance' of a small disappointment.

lingo A contemptuous term for the language of a particular set of people.

stupent In a state of stupor or amazement. Shaw has an extensive vocabulary and uses rare words with precision.

Tottenham Court Road A mixed shopping centre at the time the play was written (see map).

a drop in i.e. had taken a drop of liquor.

What about the ambassador's garden party? See the Note Taker's speech towards the end of Act 1, beginning, 'You see this creature ...'

guttersnipe Street urchin.

Monkey Brand A make of kitchen soap.

Whiteley This was a big London store, in Queensway.

By George A mild oath, presumably a contraction of 'By St George.'

off his chump Out of his mind (colloquial), a 'balmy'.

balmies Madmen (slang).

Tower of London In the old days a Royal fortress, invariably the place of execution of political prisoners.

Hounslow A West (Greater) London suburb, beyond Richmond.

fairity i.e. fair, fair play.

native woodnotes wild A quotation from Milton's *Il Penseroso*.

Wales Wales because Welsh preachers are famed for their (Celtic) eloquence.

kimono A long Japanese robe with sleeves.

By Jove! Jove was the king of the Roman gods, and the oath sounds softer to English ears than 'By God!'

Please, sir Said because Higgins had promised not to swear in front of the girl.

touch you for Get out of you.

lip Cheek, impudence (in speech).

the girls i.e. the other flower girls, her former associates.

Revision questions on Act 2

1 Describe the Flower Girl's visit to Higgins.

2 What was her reason for coming and why did Higgins keep her?

3 In what ways did Mrs Pearce request Higgins to reform his behaviour in this scene?

4 Describe the admission of Doolittle into Higgins's laboratory.

5 State in a few words the reason for Doolittle's visit.

6 Describe Doolittle's home life.

7 Describe Eliza's attire (a) when she comes in at the beginning of the scene, (b) when she rushes out at the end of the scene.

Act 3

Some months later, on his mother's at-home day, Higgins bursts into her drawing-room unexpectedly. She says that he must go, because he offends all her friends, but he tells her about Eliza and that he has asked her to call on his mother that afternoon.

Just then Mrs and Miss Eynsford Hill are announced, and they turn out to be the mother and daughter who sheltered from the rain in Covent Garden. Higgins's behaviour does not fail to earn him the reputation his mother has given him. Pickering and Freddy are shown in successively, and finally Miss Doolittle. Eliza's distinction and beauty produce such an impact on the gathered party that they rise as she enters. Freddy appears to be infatuated with her. Her conversation is at first correct, but very stilted and far from free and easy. But when her tongue is unloosed, off her prepared topics, she leads the conversation and relapses into her own racy 'Lisson Grove lingo'. Freddy and the others, at Higgins's suggestion, accept this as a new form of small talk. The climax comes when, after a hint from Higgins, she has said goodbye very courteously to all, and Freddy at the door asks her if she is 'walking across the Park' (intending to offer to accompany her). She startles the company, as Mrs Higgins's at-homes have never been startled before, with, 'Walk! Not bloody likely. I am going in a taxi.' This creates a sensation. Mrs Eynsford Hill is shocked, but Clara, her daughter, thinking that her mother is old-fashioned, brings a 'bloody' into her own conversation before she goes, to prove how up to date she is.

The Hills depart, and after they have gone Mrs Higgins tells her son frankly that Eliza's speech is not presentable, that she gives herself away in every sentence she utters, and that he and Pickering are 'a pretty pair of babies, playing with their live doll'. They rush to the defence of Eliza and their absorbing experiment, but with practical common sense Mrs Higgins points out the problem of what life Eliza will be fitted for when the experiment is over. The men will not take it seriously, whereupon Mrs Higgins has difficulty in finding words to voice her impatience with them.

at-home day The day in the week when it is understood by her friends that she will be in to any visitors who care to call for tea. In the early part of the century all ladies of the upper and upper-middle classes kept such a day.

Morris and Burne Jones William Morris (1834–96), besides being a poet, was a master designer who did much for the improvement of taste in domestic decoration. Sir Edward Burne Jones (1833–98) was associated with Morris in this work, but is better known as a painter – in rich colours. In subject and splendid colouring he showed the influence of Rossetti (see note below).

Grosvenor Gallery Opened in 1877 at 135 New Bond Street (see map). At the exhibitions of paintings there Pre-Raphaelite pictures were given prominence, and through them Burne Jones and Whistler became more widely known to the British public in general. This Gallery is not to be confused with the Grosvenor Gallery housing the private collection of the Duke of Westminster, in a wing of his town house in Park Lane (now the Grosvenor House Hotel).

Whistler An artist (1834–1903) contemporary with Burne Jones, but whose work has little in common with his. The colours in his paintings are more sombre. Shaw's remark implies that the pictures in Mrs Higgin's drawing room were in rich colours.

Cecil Lawson A landscape painter (1851–82) whose pictures had little success until his 'Minister's Garden' exhibition at the Grosvenor Galleries (1878) made him famous.

on the scale of a Rubens i.e. a very large painting. Rubens was one of the most notable of Flemish painters (1577–1640), and paintings on large canvases are characteristic of him.

Rossettian costumes i.e. costumes like those of the female figures in the paintings of Dante Gabriel Rossetti (1828–82). A Rossettian costume is a long, simple gown, high-waisted, with a girdle, and with long sleeves coming in tightly towards the wrists, the skirt falling in soft folds to the ground.

estheticism Shaw's spelling of 'aestheticism'.

bell button i.e. a push button to ring a bell (for the maid).

Chippendale chair Thomas Chippendale (1718–79) was a Yorkshire cabinet-maker who migrated to London and became fonder of designing furniture than making it, and the London furniture-makers of two hundred years ago modelled their work on his designs. Chippendale chairs were rather light in weight, had fairly broad seats, more often than not in tapestry, and the centre of the back was interestingly shaped. Often they had plain wooden arms and were not upholstered. In those days every chair was the work of an individual craftsman, even if modelled on Chippendale's design, and so it will be seen that there was a great variety in the detail – chairs did not come off the line.

Inigo Jones A famous architect (1573–1652), Surveyor-General of Royal Buildings, who built and furnished the Banqueting Hall at Whitehall, the only part of the Palace still standing. It was he who was the architect of St Paul's Church (see note p.49). Artists of past centuries specialized less than their counterparts of today and an architect might well design a palace and chairs to go in it. Such an Elizabethan chair would have a fairly broad seat. would be more ornate and heavy than a Chippendale chair, and neither as nicely proportioned nor as graceful.

between four and five If much after four it would be rather late for anyone to arrive for tea.

Ahdedo? A way of saying 'How do you do?' with an affected air of superiority (the opposite way of maltreating the English language to Eliza's).

Royal Society Great Britain's oldest learned society, for the study and promotion of natural science, granted a royal charter by Charles II. It is very influential in scientific circles, its annual summer meeting has a wide press, and practically all leading

scientists are members. The ordinary meetings are held at
Burlington House.

soirées Social evenings.

dickens Devil (slang). The word has, however, a milder effect.

burst Bout of drunkenness (or 'bust up' in slang).

Sensation It caused a sensation in the theatre too when the play
was first performed (see p.14).

forecastle The forward part of a ship under the deck where the
crew have their quarters.

my days i.e. my at-home days.

cracked i.e. crazy (crack-brained).

the sanguinary element A witty way of alluding to the word
'bloody'.

Not as long ... hands Because she knows how often Henry uses
the word himself.

Hottentot A South African race formerly occupying the region
near the Cape of Good Hope.

Beethoven One of the greatest composers (a German,
1770–1827), whose symphonies are renowned all over the world
for their imagination.

Brahms Another eminent German composer of classical music
(1833–97).

Lehar A Hungarian composer of lighter music (1870–1948) who
wrote *The Merry Widow* and other operettas.

Lionel Monckton English composer (1861–1924) and music
critic of the *Daily Telegraph*. He wrote many songs for the
musical stage.

Shakespear exhibition A Shakespeare exhibition might
include first editions of his plays, portraits of famous
Shakespearean actors, costumes worn in the plays, early theatre
programmes etc.

Revision questions on Act 3

1 Describe Mrs Higgins's drawing room.

2 'I'm sorry to say that my celebrated son has no manners.'

Do you agree with this, judging in some detail from Higgins's behaviour in this scene?

3 Show on what lines Eliza's conversation develops between her entrance and her exit.

4 What is Mrs Higgins's opinion of her son's experiment with his 'live doll'?

5 What do Pickering and Higgins say to Mrs Higgins in praise of Eliza?

Act 4

At the end of the final day in Eliza's training – a garden party, a dinner party and the opera – Eliza comes back to Higgins's laboratory in brilliant attire but wearing an almost tragic expression. Pickering assesses results and tells Higgins that he has won his bet: the experiment has been a great success. All Higgins can say is, 'Thank God it's over.'

Eliza winces as they discuss her as though she wasn't there, taking all the credit for their immense success and never giving a thought that *her* efforts have counted for anything. Furthermore, as Mrs Higgins hinted at the end of Act 3, what is to become of her now? 'You thank God it's all over, and that now you can throw me back again there do you? What am I fit for? What have you left me fit for? Where am I to go? What am I to do? Whats to become of me?' Higgins says that she may get married, or that Pickering could set her up in her florist's shop. Eliza wants to know what in her wardrobe belongs to her, as when she leaves she does not want to be accused of stealing. In a fit of anger, Higgins tells her that she may take everything except the jewels, which are hired. This is just what Eliza wanted. Higgins walks out in a rage and, left to herself,

Eliza smiles for the first time at her triumph.

Eliza goes up to her room, changes into her walking clothes and leaves the house. Outside, she meets with Freddy who admits to spending most nights outside the house. He declares his love and they embrace. A policeman arrives and moves them along. They take a taxi to Wimbledon Common.

La Fanciulla del Golden West *The Girl from the Golden West.* An opera by Giacomo Puccini, first performed in the Covent Garden Opera House in 1911 (the year before *Pygmalion*), and therefore the air would no doubt be familiar to many in the audience.

coroneted billet-doux Love letter with a crown on (Fr). He is being sarcastic, of course. In those days there were three or four postal deliveries a day in London (and other big cities), including one late in the afternoon.

tomfoolery Nonsense, playing the fool.

crisps Turns them in so that her knuckles stand out and then her nails cut into her hands.

Tosh Rubbish, nonsense (slang).

togs Clothes (slang).

millennium Golden age, lit. period of a thousand years, but used of Christ's reign on earth.

their being missing Eliza talks excellent English now!

Brighton Britain's famous seaside resort, on the south coast, just over fifty miles due south of London.

Revision question on Act 4

1 Describe Eliza's dress, expression and frame of mind as she returns from her last and greatest triumph.

2 What makes Eliza lose control of herself?

3 Why is Higgins unable to understand her feelings?

4 Do you think that in this scene Eliza is genuine or is cunningly playing a part for a purpose? Give your reasons.

Act 5

Mrs Higgins is informed by her parlour-maid that Henry and Colonel Pickering are down below, telephoning the police. She gives instructions that they are only to be shown up to the drawing-room when they have finished with the police, but that first Miss Doolittle upstairs must be told that Mr Henry and the Colonel are in the house and that she must not come down till she is sent for.

Henry then bursts in. He is in a fury as he announces that Eliza has 'bolted'. This is the reason for his telephone call to the police. Mrs Higgins shows little sympathy with him and reminds him calmly that the girl has a perfect right to leave if she so chooses. The maid then announces Mr Doolittle – 'a gentleman'. He is 'brilliantly dressed' in the latest fashion. Higgins is surprised to find that his visit has nothing to do with Eliza's disappearance. He has come to complain about being left £3,000 a year in the will of a rich American philanthropist; this is the result of a casual remark of Higgins in a letter, saying that Alfred Doolittle is the most original moralist alive. This inheritance means that Doolittle must be handed over to middle class morality. In Mrs Higgins's view it solves the problem of Eliza's future – he can provide for her.

Mrs Higgins now amazes the company by telling them that Eliza is upstairs – she came to her early in the morning after walking about all night, being frightened and angry after her brutal treatment of the night before. Higgins and Pickering defend themselves against this charge. However, Eliza is sent for and Doolittle is asked to go out of sight to soften the shock for Eliza when she comes in, so that everything will not come at once. Eliza enters, 'giving a staggeringly convincing exhibition of ease of manner'. After a first greeting she takes no notice of Higgins, but thanks

Colonel Pickering for teaching her to be a lady through his natural graces. She has, she says, quite broken off with 'the corner of Tottenham Court Road'. Just then she catches sight of her father in his fashionable outfit and screams out in her old way. Doolittle startles everyone by telling her that the reason he is dressed up is in order to marry Eliza's step-mother at St George's, Hanover Square. Middle class morality has claimed its victim, his 'poor old woman', who has been very low, dwelling on the good old days that are no more, now that she has to do what is expected by members of the middle class. They are all invited to the wedding, and all but Higgins accept.

After this Eliza and Higgins are left together for a time. Higgins tries to get her to stay with him, offering various inducements, but what she needs, she says, is 'a little kindness', and not to be 'dirt under your feet'. 'If I cant have kindness,' she says, 'I'll have independence' and so at the end of the play she sweeps off the stage giving Higgins a disdainful rebuff.

in a state i.e. in a state of excitement or fury.

bolted i.e. absconded, or – to use another similar expression – cleared off.

put the lid on me Was the end of me, stopped all my chances (slang).

acause Because.

Skilly ... Char Bydis The dustman's rendering of Scylla and Charybdis. In classical mythology Scylla was a dangerous rock in the Strait of Messina, near the Italian coast, but in avoiding it, mariners ran a great risk of being drawn into the whirlpool of Charybdis near the opposite shore. One might paraphase 'between the devil and the deep sea'.

Just the other ... language The student should refer to Act 4 to see how exaggerated this account is.

spraddling Sprawling, spreading out his legs.

St George's, Hanover Square A favourite church for society
weddings.

turned off i.e. Eliza's stepmother will not care about him when
she is married to him.

brougham A one-horse closed carriage.

Governor-General of India In those days (and until 1947) the
direct sovereignty of India was vested in the British Crown,
through a Governor-General.

Lord-Lieutenant of Ireland Similarly Ireland (Eire included)
was part of Great Britain, ruled from Westminster.

ignoramus Ignorant person.

slut Slovenly woman, slattern.

consort Accompanying (sailing with another ship).

Stilton cheese A delicious blue-veined soft cheese, named after
Stilton, in Cambridgeshire, supposedly where its manufacture
originated.

reindeer gloves Thick suede gloves made of reindeer hide.
They were fashionable for men in Edwardian times.

youve spoiled i.e. by your lack of sympathy, not by over-
indulgence (unless Mrs Higgins is being sarcastic).

Revision questions on Act 5

1 Why was Higgins upset at the beginning of this act?

2 Why was Eliza upset?

3 What was the reason for Mr Doolittle's 'very particular
call' upon Higgins?

4 Show briefly how Eliza turns the tables on Higgins in
this Act.

5 Do you think that Eliza meant the last words she said,
or do you think that she would relent and come back with
Higgins's shopping order? Give your reasons.

Epilogue

The Epilogue tells the rest of the story. Eliza marries Freddy, and after some hesitation they open a florist's shop. It does not pay at first, as they know nothing of business. However they work hard and in time it expands into a prosperous florist's and greengrocer's.

Eliza keeps in touch with Wimpole Street in spite of the shop and her own family. She is fond of her husband and loves the Colonel as a father but she persists in nagging Higgins.

Clara, on finding out that the girl who had dazzled her and whom she wished to take for a model had come from the gutter, overcomes her snobbery, begins to enjoy life and makes easy and sincere human contacts. Her conversion is helped by the puissant pen of H. G. Wells, whom she worships, and she eventually goes to work as an assistant in an old furniture shop.

Nell Gwynne A popular London actress (1650–87) who became one of the mistresses of Charles II. Their eldest son was made Duke of St Albans.

she became i.e. Eliza (not Nell Gwynne).

Landor. Walter Savage Landor (1775–1864), a well known English critic and prose writer. The actual remark was 'Love is a secondary passion in those who love most'.

Pygmalion See note p.49.

predestinate Pre-ordained, predestined (as if by fate).

Nietzsche An original German philosopher (1844–1900) whose works were translated into English and who had a great influence in England in his day.

biting off more than they can chew i.e. undertaking more than they can manage.

cross i.e. duty. See note on 'feather-weight cross', p.54.

déclassée Taken out of her class (Fr.), 'disclassed' as Shaw says a little way below, coining a word of his own.

Nietzschean ... evil Referring to Nietzsche's work *Beyond Good and Evil*. 'Transcendence' means 'rising higher than', or using the word in the title of the book) 'rising *beyond*'.

four thousand Three thousand in Act 5. Does Shaw mean to imply that he picked up an extra thousand pounds as lecturing 'expenses'?

because Freddy ... any to spend This might equally well have been given as a reason for his squandering the money.

Mr H. G. Wells An English novelist (1866–1946), spokesman for the 'little man' in novels such as *Kipps* and *The History of Mr Polly*.

Acts of the Apostles H. G. Wells is seen as an apostle of the modern age. Shaw was impressed by the ideas of H. G. Wells, another daring thinker of his own day and generation.

West Kensington A good middle-class area in the years preceding the First World War (1914–18).

Epsom See note p.51.

this exquisite apparition i.e. Eliza.

the angle of view ... social structure As in *Kipps*.

conviction of sin i.e. the sin of snobbery.

General Booth William Booth, founder of the Salvation Army (1829–1912).

Gypsy Smith Rodney Smith (1860–1947), a famous evangelist, a convert of General William Booth at a Salvation Army meeting in Whitechapel Road in 1877. So called because he was a gipsy – born in a gipsy tent of gipsy parents.

on that tack i.e. in those affairs (colloquial).

Glasworthy A famous novelist and dramatist (1867–1933), whose novels were to be documentary to the times (e.g. the depiction of the industrial world in *Strife*). His novels under the collective title of *The Forsyte Saga* are very popular. They depict the English middle class, and 'the vanity of Largelady Park' – the lower middle class which tries to ape the more affluent class; there is also some nostalgia as Galsworthy was born into this class.

ineptitudes Absurd actions.

scutcheon Lit. shield bearing the family coat of arms, here a metaphor for the family reputation and position.

a railway station ... Museum Victoria Station.

Porson Richard Porson (1759–1808), regius professor of Greek at Cambridge.

Bentley Richard Bentley (1662–1742), Master of Trinity College, Cambridge, a classical scholar renowned all over Europe in his day.

Unfortunately he knew nothing else The stock criticism of grammar schools of that day, especially the old-fashioned ones.

Balbus ... three parts Information he would read in his Latin textbook at school. Caesar's *Commentaries on the Gallic War* are a common school textbook.

did not carry ... business Shaw's dig at the uselessness of contemporary education.

polytechnic A Polytechnic school is one where many varied subjects (usually with a technical bias) are taught. The reference is undoubtedly to the well-known classes organized by the London Polytechnic Institution.

London School of Economics One of the schools (i.e. departments) of the University of London, situated in Houghton Street, Aldwych (see map p.4).

Dickensian by Charles Dickens, celebrated English novelist (1812–70).

London School i.e. attendance at the London School of Economics.

Kew Gardens Celebrated botanical gardens (open to the public) up the River Thames on the south side, west of Kew Bridge. Now in Greater London.

caligraphy (Usually spelt 'calligraphy'); penmanship, handwriting, generally in a context implying *beautiful* handwriting.

Italian hand The form of cursive handwriting used in this country (but not script writing), America and most of Western Europe (though not in Germany).

congenitally i.e. she was made like that and could not alter it.

asparagus A table delicacy for the well-to-do. As poor people did not relish it there was no price-cutting necessary in its sale.

like anything An unusually 'common' simile for Shaw.

Galatea A nymph of Classical mythology (one of the Nereides), in love with Acis, who was killed before she could marry him.

General Questions

1 Write an essay on the stage history of *Pygmalion*.

2 Analyse the construction of *Pygmalion*, act by act.

3 It has been said that the play is badly constructed because what ought to be the climax – the success of Eliza at the garden party or the dinner party – is left out, so far as the stage is concerned. Do you agree?

4 Would you prefer *Pygmalion* without the Epilogue or do you find it helpful?

5 Which of Higgins's qualities do you (a) admire, (b) detest the most? Give your reasons.

6 Write a full character study of Eliza Doolittle.

7 'Why did you take my independence from me? Why did I give it up?' What are the answers to these questions in your judgement?

8 In the Preface to *Pygmalion* Shaw says, 'Finally, and for the encouragement of people troubled with accents that cut them off from all high employment, I may add that the change wrought by Profesor Higgins in the flower girl is neither impossible nor uncommon.' Do you think that the change wrought in Shaw's flower-girl is exaggerated? Illustrate your answer from the play.

9 'In spite of all her improvement in speech we always feel that Eliza Doolittle is in her heart of hearts the flower-girl' (Patrick Braybrooke). Do you feel it? Give reasons for your answer.

10 Do you think that it was cruel to take Eliza from her class and make her live in another? Say why.

11 What part is played in *Pygmalion* by (a) Alfred Doolittle, (b) Mrs Pearce, (c) Clara Eynsford Hill?

12 Can you believe that Doolittle would be disappointed at coming into £3000 a year? Comment on the credibility of his character.

13 Why did Eliza like Pickering?

14 Comment on Shaw's English style.

15 Point out any places in the play where it sounds as if Shaw is addressing the audience.

16 What advantages are there in the exact location of the scenes of a play, e.g. St Paul's Church, 27A Wimpole Street?

17 Write on Shaw's use of contrast.

18 Comment on the nature of Shaw's humour.

19 Point out the explicit nature of some of the stage directions in the play.

Pan study aids Titles published in the Brodie's Notes series

W. H. Auden Selected Poetry

Jane Austen Emma Mansfield Park Northanger Abbey Persuasion
Pride and Prejudice

Anthologies of Poetry Ten Twentieth Century Poets
The Metaphysical Poets The Poet's Tale

Samuel Beckett Waiting for Godot

Arnold Bennett The Old Wives' Tale

William Blake Songs of Innocence and Experience

Robert Bolt A Man for All Seasons

Harold Brighouse Hobson's Choice

Charlotte Brontë Jane Eyre

Emily Brontë Wuthering Heights

Robert Browning Selected Poetry

John Bunyan The Pilgrim's Progress

Geoffrey Chaucer (parallel texts editions) The Franklin's Tale
The Knight's Tale The Miller's Tale The Nun's Priest's Tale
The Pardoner's Tale Prologue to the Canterbury Tales
The Wife of Bath's Tale

Richard Church Over the Bridge

John Clare Selected Poetry and Prose

Samuel Taylor Coleridge Selected Poetry and Prose

Wilkie Collins The Woman in White

William Congreve The Way of the World

Joseph Conrad The Nigger of the Narcissus & Youth
The Secret Agent

Charles Dickens Bleak House David Copperfield Dombey and Son
Great Expectations Hard Times Little Dorrit Oliver Twist
Our Mutual Friend A Tale of Two Cities

Gerald Durrell My Family and Other Animals

George Eliot Middlemarch The Mill on the Floss Silas Marner

T. S. Eliot Murder in the Cathedral Selected Poems

J. G. Farrell The Siege of Krishnapur

Henry Fielding Joseph Andrews

F. Scott Fitzgerald The Great Gatsby

E. M. Forster Howards End A Passage to India
Where Angels Fear to Tread

William Golding Lord of the Flies The Spire

Oliver Goldsmith Two Plays of Goldsmith: She Stoops to Conquer;
The Good Natured Man

Graham Greene Brighton Rock The Power and the Glory
The Quiet American

Thom Gunn and Ted Hughes Selected Poems

Thomas Hardy Chosen Poems of Thomas Hardy Far from the
Madding Crowd Jude the Obscure The Mayor of Casterbridge
Return of the Native Tess of the D'Urbervilles The Trumpet-Major

L. P. Hartley The Go-Between The Shrimp and the Anemone

Joseph Heller Catch-22

Ernest Hemingway For Whom the Bell Tolls
The Old Man and the Sea

Barry Hines A Kestrel for a Knave

Gerard Manley Hopkins Poetry and Prose of Gerard Manley
Hopkins

Aldous Huxley Brave New World

Henry James Washington Square

Ben Jonson The Alchemist Volpone

James Joyce A Portrait of the Artist as a Young Man

John Keats Selected Poems and Letters of John Keats

Ken Kesey One Flew Over the Cuckoo's Nest

Rudyard Kipling Kim
D. H. Lawrence The Rainbow Selected Tales Sons and Lovers
Harper Lee To Kill a Mocking-bird

Laurie Lee As I Walked out One Midsummer Morning
Cider with Rosie

Thomas Mann Death in Venice & Tonio Kröger

Christopher Marlowe Doctor Faustus Edward the Second

W. Somerset Maugham Of Human Bondage

Arthur Miller The Crucible Death of a Salesman

John Milton A Choice of Milton's Verse Comus and Samson
Agonistes Paradise Lost, I, II

Sean O'Casey Juno and the Paycock The Shadow of a Gunman and
The Plough and the Stars

George Orwell Animal Farm 1984

John Osborne Luther

Alexander Pope Selected Poetry
Siegfried Sassoon Memoirs of a Fox-Hunting Man
Peter Shaffer The Royal Hunt of the Sun
William Shakespeare Antony and Cleopatra As You Like It
Coriolanus Hamlet Henry IV (Part I) Henry IV (Part II) Henry V
Julius Caesar King Lear King Richard III Love's Labour's Lost
Macbeth Measure for Measure The Merchant of Venice
A Midsummer Night's Dream Much Ado about Nothing Othello
Richard II Romeo and Juliet The Sonnets The Taming of the Shrew
The Tempest Twelfth Night The Winter's Tale
G. B. Shaw Androcles and the Lion Arms and the Man
Caesar and Cleopatra The Doctor's Dilemma Pygmalion Saint Joan
Richard Sheridan Plays of Sheridan: The Rivals; The Critic;
The School for Scandal
John Steinbeck The Grapes of Wrath Of Mice and Men & The
Pearl
Tom Stoppard Rosencrantz and Guildenstern are Dead
J. M. Synge The Playboy of the Western World
Jonathan Swift Gulliver's Travels
Alfred Tennyson Selected Poetry
William Thackeray Vanity Fair
Flora Thompson Lark Rise to Candleford
Dylan Thomas Under Milk Wood
Anthony Trollope Barchester Towers
Mark Twain Huckleberry Finn
Keith Waterhouse Billy Liar
Evelyn Waugh Decline and Fall Scoop
H. G. Wells The History of Mr Polly
John Webster The White Devil
Oscar Wilde The Importance of Being Earnest
Virginia Woolf To the Lighthouse
William Wordsworth The Prelude (Books 1, 2)
John Wyndham The Chrysalids
W. B. Yeats Selected Poetry

Australian Titles

George Johnston My Brother Jack
Thomas Keneally The Chant of Jimmy Blacksmith
Ray Lawler Summer of the Seventeenth Doll
Henry Lawson The Bush Undertaker & Selected Short Stories
Ronald McKie The Mango Tree
Kenneth Slessor Selected Poems
Ralph Stow The Merry-Go-Round in the Sea To the Islands
Patrick White The Tree of Man
David Williamson The Removalists